USING COMPUTER SCIENCE IN
CONSTRUCTION
»CAREERS«

CARLA MOONEY

Rosen
YA™
New York

Published in 2019 by The Rosen Publishing Group, Inc.
29 East 21st Street, New York, NY 10010

Library of Congress Cataloging-in-Publication Data

Names: Mooney, Carla, 1970– author.
Title: Using computer science in construction careers / Carla Mooney.
Description: New York : Rosen Publishing, 2019. | Series: Coding your passion | Includes bibliographical references and index. | Audience: Grades 7–12.
Identifiers: LCCN 2018014239| ISBN 9781508183914 (library bound) | ISBN 9781508183907 (pbk.)
Subjects: LCSH: Building—Data processing—Juvenile literature.
Classification: LCC TH438.13 .M66 2019 | DDC 624.0285—dc23
LC record available at https://lccn.loc.gov/2018014239

Manufactured in the United States of America

CONTENTS

INTRODUCTION

On the University of Washington campus, the new computer science building is scheduled to soon open its doors. The 135,000-square-foot (12,542-square-meter) building will house classrooms, lab space, workrooms, seminar rooms, a 250-person lecture hall, and conference facilities. Even though construction on the building is not complete, the school community can virtually tour the new campus building through a simple app on their smartphones. The construction company in charge of the project, Mortenson Construction, announced that it had developed a new augmented reality (AR) app, which uses technology to superimpose computer-generated images onto real images. It can be used to help students, teachers, and other community members "see" the new computer science building before it's complete.

To use the app, users simply point their phones to the campus construction site to experience a life-like digital representation of the building. Through the app, users can explore the building's exterior in AR. They then move inside to an immersive virtual reality (VR) experience, or simulated reality, in several areas, including the main lobby, a workroom, a robotics lab, and several offices.

Marc Kinsman led Mortenson's in-house immersive-technology team in developing the app. Kinsman

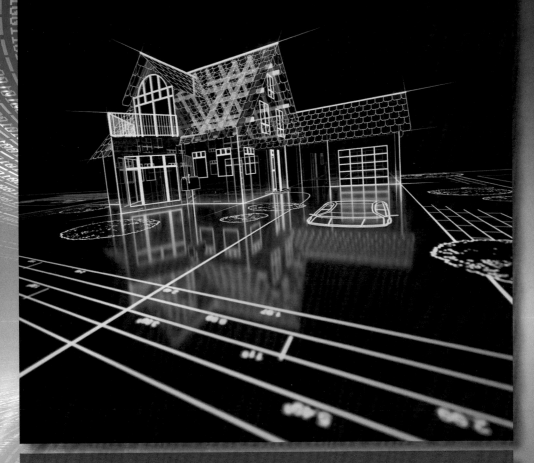

With virtual and augmented reality technologies, users can view a
building project from all angles, keeping an eye out for any design
changes needed before construction starts.

said in an article on the company's website that the technology:

> presents a tremendous opportunity to engage the public, and to build excitement around campus. AR and VR represent a vast improvement over traditional public engagement methods like flyers, fencing signage, or a website. We are scratching the surface of what's possible.

Like Mortenson, today's modern construction companies are increasingly using technology and computers in their operations. Construction management software, building information modeling, virtual reality, and cloud computing are just a few examples of technologies that are having a significant impact on the construction industry. They help these companies become more efficient, increase profits, reduce errors and waste, and improve safety.

Projects are becoming larger and much more complex. "Innovations...have enormous potential to speed up project progress, improve accuracy and safety," said Geno Armstrong from the strategic advisory firm KPMG in a recent article posted on the Connect and Construct website.

As technology and computers change the way the construction industry operates, they also create new opportunities for people with an interest in computer science and construction. Young people entering the construction industry today expect the latest technologies. "Estimating, project managing, (and) scheduling using state of the art tools (are) all they've ever known. There's pressure from within the company to automate and adopt new technologies. You can't compete otherwise," said Christian Burger, principal and owner of Burger Consulting Group, Inc., an IT construction industry consulting firm, in a recent article on Business.com.

In the construction industry, there are many different computer science career specialties that students can pursue. Construction companies employ software developers, building information modeling (BIM) managers, cloud computing professionals, web developers, and more. With so many opportunities, careers that merge construction and computer science can fit many backgrounds and interests.

CHAPTER ONE

CODING AND CONSTRUCTION

Across the country, people live and work in towering skyscrapers and sprawling factory complexes. They drive on multi-lane highways, through concrete tunnels, and over long bridges. They shop in suburban shopping malls and on city streets lined by storefronts, coffee shops, and restaurants. At night, they return home to multifloor apartment buildings or houses in suburban neighborhoods. All around, the construction industry shapes and builds the places where people live and work every day.

A LOOK AT THE CONSTRUCTION INDUSTRY

The construction industry is a sector of the economy that is involved with building, maintaining, and repairing buildings and other structures. The industry

During the design phase of a construction project, team members need to collaborate. Software can help them do this more effectively.

produces houses, apartments, factories, offices, schools, roads, bridges, and more. In addition to building new structures, construction companies are involved in preparing sites, performing maintenance, and updating existing structures.

Traditionally, the construction industry is divided into three main sub-sectors: the construction of buildings, infrastructure construction (roads, highways, and bridges), and specialty trades. The construction of buildings subsector includes buildings of all types, from residential homes and farms to industrial factories and multistory high-rise office buildings. The infrastructure subsector covers construction other than buildings, such as highways, streets, bridges, sewers, railroads, and more. Specialty trades include activities related to building construction, such as painting, electrical work, plumbing, and carpentry.

A construction project is usually coordinated by a general contractor who specializes in a particular type of construction, such as residential homes or commercial buildings. General contractors are responsible for every part of a project, unless a portion of the work is specifically excluded from their contract. General contractors often subcontract parts of a project to other specialty contractors. Even when using subcontractors, the general contractor is still responsible for the entire project—for getting it done on time and on budget.

The construction industry is an important part of the US economy. It currently employs more than seven million workers in the United States, according to the US Department of Labor's Bureau of Labor Statistics (BLS). That number is projected to increase to more than 7.5 million jobs by 2026.

MERGING CONSTRUCTION AND COMPUTER SCIENCE

The modern construction industry is using technology and computers in their operations. This growth has opened the door for people who are interested in working in the construction industry and also have an interest in computer science and coding. Companies need qualified information technology professionals, software developers, and internet-savvy employees who can work in a digital environment. Performing a variety of roles, these professionals create innovative ways for construction companies to improve their operations and beat the competition.

A project team member reviews a digital floorplan on a laptop. Using construction software, the worker can easily make changes.

Having strong computer science skills is essential for most construction technology careers. Many people working in construction technology have a computer science degree. A few have degrees in engineering or construction. No matter their degree, people working in construction need to be knowledgeable in construction management systems, cloud computing, building information modeling, and web technology. Knowledge of programming languages such as Perl, Python, Ruby, Java, C/C++, and HTML are valuable.

THE ART OF 3D PRINTING

Another technology ready to make a big impact on the construction industry is 3D printing. Also known as additive manufacturing, 3D printing is the process of making three-dimensional solid objects from a digital file. To make an object, the 3D printer adds layer after layer of a material until a solid three-dimensional physical object is formed. Companies have used 3D printing to make car parts, smartphone cases, fashion accessories, artificial organs, and more.

In recent years, engineers have been experimenting with 3D printing in construction. Using special super-size printers and a concrete and composite mixture, they are experimenting with making components for building homes—and even entire homes. The concrete mixture is much thicker than traditional concrete, which enables it to support itself as it sets.

In the future, 3D printing may revolutionize the construction industry. Components made via 3D printing use less material than components made with traditional concrete. They can also be hollow, which allows building services to be placed right inside the building's structural elements. 3D printing may also expand the types of forms architects can use, freeing them to design more creatively.

Some firms are experimenting with using 3D printing to create entire structures. Recently, a Dutch 3D printing company began to work on printing a full-scale steel bridge. When complete, the 3D printed bridge will be installed in downtown Amsterdam. A Chinese company recently announced that it had made an entire concrete mansion in 45 days. The company constructed the building's frame and installed plumbing and electrical writing. Then it printed the structure using a concrete mixture and a computer-controlled 3D printer. While 3D printing of buildings is not yet ready to go mainstream, the possibilities are exciting.

In addition to technical skills, construction employers are looking for people who have other skills in business and project management. For many construction industry careers, the ability to work well with other people and communicate is critical. Many positions require a person to think innovatively to solve problems and meet customer needs.

PURSUING A CAREER IN CONSTRUCTION AND COMPUTER SCIENCE

People who are interested in a computer science career in the construction industry should take classes to give them solid technical computer and programming skills. Some people choose to get a computer-related degree from a four-year college or

Students can take classes in writing code and other computer skills that they will need as computer science professionals.

university. Others who have degrees in another field attend special coding boot camps or technology-focused graduate programs. For some specialties, earning a certificate is a good way to show that a person has the skills needed for the career.

In addition to taking classes, people interested in a computer science career related to construction can take other steps to learn more about the industry. Joining a construction industry professional organization can help a person network and make contacts. Some companies offer internships to students. These internships give students experience working for a particular company or industry. Reading business and technology publications can help students keep up to date on the latest innovations in the field.

CHAPTER TWO

CONSTRUCTION MANAGEMENT SOFTWARE

Today's construction projects are more complex than ever and require the skills of many different people. Construction companies work hand-in-hand with architects, subcontractors, and others. Many projects also use dozens of subcontractors, each of which specializes in a specific part of the project, such as electrical work or roofing. Even within a construction company, different departments are involved in a project, including design, safety, finance, materials, procurement, operations, and more. With so many people working together, a successful project depends on strong project management and organization. Everyone involved must work together efficiently to ensure the project is finished on time and on budget.

MAKING PROJECT MANAGEMENT EASIER

Increasingly, construction companies are using construction management software to help them

Construction management software helps managers communicate with others and better monitor and track workflows on site.

organize projects, people, and workflows. Companies across all segments of the construction industry are using this technology for residential, commercial, and industrial construction projects. Construction management software helps companies manage every detail of a project, from estimating the materials needed to scheduling personnel and equipment at the job site. The software gives them tools for estimating and tracking project costs, forecasting and budgeting, communicating with clients and subcontractors, managing documents, and tracking a project's progress. Because many software packages are cloud based, people working on the project can access the software from anywhere at any time as long as they have an internet connection.

Using construction management software has helped many construction companies save time and money. According to a recent survey by software research service Capterra, four out of five construction project managers reported that using construction software allowed them to complete projects in less time. Spending less time on a project translates into lower costs and less waste. Construction software also saves companies time and money by using streamlined digital documentation. According to the Capterra survey, more than one-third of construction managers spend more than two hours each day on project documentation. Using software to streamline documentation can free up these managers for other tasks and reduce printing costs, in some cases by more than 50 percent.

For many companies, the estimating, project planning, and job costing features in construction management software can help them win projects and increase sales. In the Capterra survey, 77 percent of users reported they had experienced an increase in project proposals won since they had begun using construction software. As the companies won more projects, sales also increased, in some cases more than 51 percent.

When building the Ruth Mulan Chu Chao Center on the Harvard Business School campus in Boston, construction firm Lee Kennedy Co. Inc. (LKCo) relied on construction management software to coordinate the project. The Chao Center is a 90,000 square-foot (8,361 square-meter), mixed-use facility that includes

Construction management software enabled builders to construct the Ruth Mulan Chu Chao Center on the Harvard Business School campus.

meeting, classroom, office, and dining spaces. Adam Settino, virtual design and construction manager at LKCo, says that construction software allowed his team to work more effectively with subcontractors and the project's architect. The team was better able to quickly and effectively resolve any issues as they arose. "Whenever we encounter a clash—a duct or pipe hitting a beam, for example—our MEP [mechanical, electrical, and plumbing] coordinator will mark up the model in [the construction software] and send it to the subcontractor," said Settino in a case study on the software company's website. "If the subcontractor can't resolve the issue because there's no way to reroute the component, we send a link to the same view to the architect. They review the model within [the construction software] and see if the design can be modified." Settino added, "We've had a lot of coordination like this on the Chao Center project, and it's helping us to solve problems faster."

MAKING REAL-TIME DECISIONS

For the Murphy Company, a national mechanical contractor, using construction management software helped them get faster and better access to critical information. Old software systems produced monthly reports, providing information that was weeks old. By the time management received the information, it was usually too late to address any job or customer issues that had arisen. After installing PENTA construction management software, Murphy executives were able to get instant access to real-time information. According to Chris Carter, Murphy's vice president of service, real-time data was critical because management needed to know how the business was operating at that moment. Having the information to determine what was happening in real-time on job sites allowed management to act more effectively and make better decisions that improved profitability and made customers happier. Since implementing PENTA, the Murphy Company has been able to double their business volume without adding significant administrative expense.

DEVELOPING CONSTRUCTION SOFTWARE

Software developers design computer programs. Some create the applications that allow people to perform specific tasks on a computer or a mobile device. Others work on the systems that run the devices and computer networks. In the construction industry, software developers create the applications and platforms needed to run construction management software and other construction technology.

Typically, software developers design, test, and develop software that meets customer needs. Often,

A software developer works on his laptop to create the applications and software used by companies in the construction industry.

developers begin by talking with customers to see what they need and how they plan to use the software. Through these discussions and other research, software developers determine the core functions required in the software program. They must also determine other user requirements such as security and performance. With this information, developers design the program. They give detailed instructions to programmers who write and test the program code.

In some companies, software developers write the code themselves. If the resulting application does not work as intended, software developers tweak the design to fix the problems. After the application is released, developers may continue to improve it with upgrades and maintenance.

BUILDING A CAREER AS A SOFTWARE DEVELOPER

Most software developers have at least a bachelor's degree in computer science, software engineering, or a related field from a four-year college or university. Although not all developers write code, students should also take classes to develop strong software computer programming skills. Even after they graduate from college, software developers must continue to hone their computer skills and stay current on new tools and programming languages.

Many students complete an internship at a software company to gain hands-on experience in software development. Some people enter the field by

Communication skills are important. A software developer explains how a new application works to those who will be using it on the company's next building project.

first working as computer programmers. As they gain experience, they take on more responsibility and can eventually become software developers.

In addition to strong computer skills, several additional skills are important for people working in this career. Software developers for the construction industry should be knowledgeable in the industry so that they can understand their company and customer needs. Developers should also be creative, have good analytical skills, and be detail oriented. A good software developer can analyze customer needs and develop a creative solution to meet those needs. Developers should have excellent communication and interpersonal skills. Many developers work closely with others on a team. They must be able to communicate effectively with team members, partly because they often have to explain how the software works to coworkers and customers.

THE JOB OUTLOOK

The job outlook for software developers is strong. According to the Bureau of Labor Statistics' *Occupational Outlook Handbook*, employment of software developers is projected to grow 24 percent by 2026. This rate of growth is much faster than the average of all occupations. The main driver behind this employment growth is an increasing demand for computer software. In addition, the need for new applications on mobile devices, such as smartphones and tablets, will also increase the demand for application software developers.

Concerns over security could result in the need for more security software to protect computer networks and applications, particularly as more project management applications are being offered over the internet. Candidates who have strong skills in the most up-to-date programming tools and languages will have the best prospects for landing a good software development job for the construction industry.

CHAPTER THREE

CONSTRUCTION AND THE CLOUD

Construction companies are using more technology every day, from construction management software to creating digital 3D models of projects. At the same time, project teams are often spread out geographically. Some team members work at the home office, while others spend the day at construction sites. With people spread out in different locations, getting everyone access to critical data, communication networks, and software applications can be a challenge. In order to work efficiently and effectively, workers need a way to access their data and communication networks no matter where they are working.

WORKING TOGETHER IN THE CLOUD

To connect a mobile construction team, many companies are implementing a cloud computing solution. Cloud computing is the delivery of

A blueprint for an office building construction project appears in 3D and can be accessed by team members through the cloud, no matter where they are physically located.

computing services, such as servers, storage, databases, networking, and software, over the internet. Simply put, instead of keeping computer hardware and software on a server in the home office, a company hires a service provider to handle it for them offsite. The cloud provider maintains the necessary server and storage hardware that processes and stores the company's information. When the company needs its information or needs to use an application, they can simply access it over the internet.

Construction companies can benefit from cloud computing because it makes accessing a company's data and software much easier. In construction, workers and job sites change constantly. At the same time, workers in the main office need to have current information to process payroll, bill customers, pay invoices, and plan work flows. Before cloud computing, computing was handled in-house by company hardware and software that could be accessed from only specific locations. Workers in the field would have to come back to the home office to access or update data. With cloud computing, workers can get the software and information they need wherever they can access the internet. They can back up information and documents in the cloud and use cloud-based software platforms to collaborate with team members in different locations. Being able to access paperwork and data from a laptop, tablet, or smartphone, without making a trip back to the office, can also save time and make employees more productive. Additionally, the cloud provider provides backup services, which protect the company from losing important documents in the event of a natural disaster, employee mistake, or even a spilled cup of coffee.

Cloud computing also improves communication. Managers can supervise workers from different locations with communication apps and software programs. For companies that do not have a centralized office, employees in different locations can connect over the internet, saving time and money. Bills, budgets, and other documents can be emailed and received in only a few minutes. Using cloud-based services to communicate also leaves an electronic paper trail that can be saved in case

Using a tablet computer, an architect reviews building plans and sends emails while at a construction site, connecting to company servers and communication networks via the cloud.

of any problems in the future. And as a company's computing needs change, cloud storage can easily be increased or decreased.

For employees at construction company True Value Homes (TVH), cloud computing has made their jobs easier and they have become more efficient. Before cloud computing, TVH employees working on multiple sites had to travel to the company's corporate office to update project information and process data using the company's computer systems. Employees often carried large amounts of paperwork into the corporate

WHY IS IT CALLED THE CLOUD?

There's been a lot of talk in the IT community about "the cloud." What exactly is the cloud and where did it come from? Traditionally, engineers design computer networks using drawings or diagrams. In these diagrams, computers that are connected on the network are connected via a line. The diagram's lines represent cables and other hard-wired connections. Switches and servers within a network are also often connected this way.

When one network connects to another, engineers often represent an external network with a drawing of a cloud. The internet is simply an external network that provides services outside of a company's internal network and hardware. That is why many services provided over the internet are called cloud services.

office to get the necessary approvals and processing. When they transitioned computing services to the cloud, TVH gave approved employees access to data and applications through a secure internet connection.

Today, TVH's 500 users update information and use the system through web-based applications. Arun Nehru, TVH's director, in an article on the Sage.com website said:

> We want to make sure that our employees get the best out of their workplace. What we are telling employees is that [wherever you need to work], the applications are available—from office, home, or outside. They need not come to [the] office to work.

WORKING IN CLOUD COMPUTING

For a person interested in cloud computing, there are several common career paths. Cloud architects design and oversee an organization's overall cloud computing strategy. They plan how a company will move existing systems to the cloud, as well as design and manage new cloud systems and applications. Cloud architects are always looking forward to the future and thinking about what a company's cloud strategy will be a few years in the future and how to prepare the company for future changes.

Once a company is using the cloud, administrators manage and monitor the organization's cloud platforms. They configure the management service and make sure everything is running smoothly. When problems arise, administrators develop solutions and resolve issues. Additionally, many companies have custom software applications designed specifically for cloud usage. Cloud application developers design and deploy software that is used in the cloud.

For any organization, keeping sensitive data and systems secure is a top priority. Cloud security managers work to ensure the safety of an organization's cloud environment. They design, execute, and maintain a security strategy for a company's cloud infrastructure. They constantly monitor the cloud systems for security threats and risks. They use security tools such as encryption, access control, and multifactor authentication to prevent unauthorized users from accessing the company's cloud systems and information.

HOW TO BECOME A CLOUD PROFESSIONAL

Most cloud professionals have at least a bachelor's degree in computer science, software engineering, or a related field from a four-year college or university. Additionally, people who want to work in cloud computing should also gain expertise in one or more of the core cloud platforms, such as Amazon Web Services, Google Cloud Platform, and Microsoft Azure. Earning a certification in one or more of these platforms can demonstrate proficiency to potential employers.

Cloud professionals often need to build, deploy, and manage a variety of cloud applications. To do so, students should also take classes to develop strong

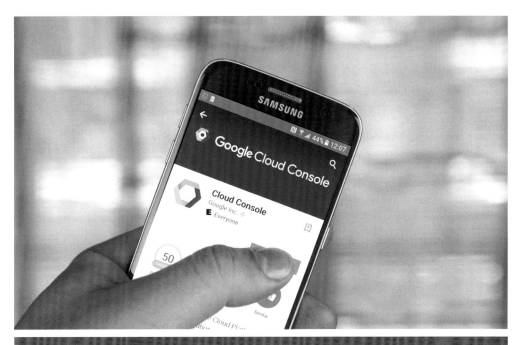

The Google Cloud Console app can be accessed on a smartphone. The app allows users to run the Google Cloud Platform directly on an Android phone or tablet.

software computer programming skills. Programming languages such as Perl, Python, and Ruby are commonly used in cloud programming. In addition, experience with Developmental Operations, or DevOps, a method of software development, is a highly valuable skill in cloud computing.

For students interested in careers in cloud security, obtaining a security certification such as the Certified Information Systems Security Professional (CISSP) is valuable. Earning the CISSP certification demonstrates proficiency in various cloud computing security areas.

Even after they graduate from college, cloud professionals must continue to develop their computer skills and stay current on new tools and programming languages. Many people enter the field by first working in another information technology position. As they gain experience in cloud computing, either on the job or through training or certification programs, they can eventually move into a cloud professional position.

THE JOB OUTLOOK

The job outlook for cloud professionals is strong. According to the Bureau of Labor Statistics' *Occupational Outlook Handbook*, employment of computer and information technology occupations, which includes cloud professionals, is projected to grow 13 percent by 2026. This rate of growth is faster than the average growth rate of all occupations.

The main driver behind this employment growth is an increasing demand for professionals with cloud computing, big data, and information security skills. "The demand for people way outweighs the supply," said David Linthicum, the senior vice president of Cloud Technology Partners, in an article for *Business Insider*. "It's very similar to when the internet exploded in the late nineties. We're seeing the same patterns in the cloud." Candidates who have strong skills in the most up-to-date cloud platforms, programming, and software development technologies will have the best prospects for landing a good cloud-related professional job in the construction industry.

CHAPTER FOUR

BUILDING INFORMATION MODELING

O ne of the hottest technology trends is building information modeling, also known as BIM. For years, designers and builders have used drawings and models to collaborate in the planning, design, and construction phases of a building or infrastructure project. With BIM, companies have gone beyond physical drawings and models. They are using technology to create and manage all of the information about a project in one place, from before construction begins until long after it ends. BIM allows a team of architects, engineers, and contractors to work together to design and construct a building.

MORE THAN A MODEL

BIM is a software-based tool that allows a project team to create a 3D design of a building on a computer and then check and solve any design

A man uses Autodesk building information modeling architectural drawings on an iPad at a construction site in Virginia.

conflicts. More than just a model, the BIM process allows every member of a project team to use the same database and view the same virtual model. The BIM 3D model includes every physical element (windows, roof, and walls) and functional system (HVAC, plumbing, and electrical) of the building.

Using the BIM model, the team can identify any errors or conflicts between elements before construction begins in the field. For example, a BIM model might reveal that the original design calls for an air duct to run straight into a concrete column. If identified during construction, this conflict could be time-consuming and costly to fix. However, using the BIM model, the team can identify the problem and rework the design before construction begins.

Team members can also use the model to test and analyze proposed changes during the design phase. BIM is a way for team members to collaborate, making the most use of the tools that the software offers.

In addition, the BIM process combines all of the information about various building systems into the master BIM model. Objects in a BIM model can be linked to other information such as product manuals, specifications, photos, and warranty details. When the project is completed, the building manager can use the model and its information to more effectively manage the building.

When architecture firm Gensler was designing the Shanghai Tower in China, employees used BIM to help with the design process. For example, the tower's complex elevator and staircase system was developed using BIM. Michael Concannon, regional digital design director at Gensler, and BIM manager on the project, said in a recent article posted on Engineering.com:

> Because it was three-dimensional, we were able to see where all of our clearances were and very quickly go through many iterations of optimal ways to do what is really a very complicated elevatoring system for a building that tall to reduce it to as tight a core as possible to be as efficient as possible.

Architecture firm Gensler used building information modeling software when designing the Shanghai Tower in China, the tallest building in Shanghai.

WORKING AS A BIM MANAGER

BIM managers coordinate the BIM process for construction projects. They help the team successfully work together. Often BIM managers oversee BIM engineers and specialists to develop and update a 3D model of a project. BIM managers develop and implement the BIM workflow, define the information required in the model, and communicate it to team members. They oversee the installation and maintenance of BIM software and help train users. Once the team is using BIM software, the manager oversees the BIM model and makes sure the model's

An architect works from her home computer and reviews design plans using BIM software. Any changes she makes can be instantly viewed by other team members.

elements are accurate and it is being used properly. BIM managers may also analyze and troubleshoot any issues that emerge.

Patrick Mitchell is a BIM Lead for Robertson Partnership Homes. In his role, Mitchell is responsible for introducing team members to the technology and business processes used in the modern construction industry. This includes the use of BIM processes and 3D modeling of projects. Mitchell enjoys the variety and challenges he finds every day as a BIM manager in the construction industry. "Every project and

BIM VS. CAD

While BIM and CAD (computer-aided design) are software tools used in the construction industry, they have some differences. CAD is primarily used by engineers to design parts, tools, or an entire project such as bridge. CAD allows engineers to create higher-quality drawings for products, more quickly. It replaces manual drawing with an automated process. Engineers use CAD software to design an object in 3D, create 2D drawings and schematics, and then edit the design. BIM software is similar to CAD, but the difference is that all of its tools are specifically meant for designing a building. BIM software includes both 2D and 3D tools to create construction documents and visualizations. While CAD can be used in any industry, BIM software is generally only used in construction.

contract has its own personality which keeps things interesting. I can be working on a housing project one week and a hospital the next," he said in an interview on GoConstruct.org.

HOW TO BECOME A BIM MANAGER

Most BIM managers hold a bachelor's or master's degree in engineering, construction, or a related field from a four-year college or university. Additionally, people who want to become a BIM manager should have experience in the construction industry and knowledge of the BIM process.

People interested in BIM careers should prepare by earning a bachelor's or master's degree and taking a variety of classes to develop their communication and leadership skills.

While they are generally not responsible for a construction project's design, BIM managers should have a basic understanding of the design and modeling process. Having good computer skills and being able to work with a variety of software programs is also a must. Students should take classes or gain on-the-job experience in design modeling and 3D and BIM software such as AutoCAD, Revit Architecture, and Navisworks. Earning a certification in one or more of these platforms can demonstrate proficiency to potential employers.

Throughout their careers, BIM managers must continue to develop their computer skills and stay current on new technologies. Many people enter the field by first working in another architectural, engineering, construction management, or CAD position. As they gain experience in BIM processes, they can eventually move into a BIM manager position.

In addition to technical skills, BIM managers have superior written and verbal communication skills. To be successful, they must be able to work with all members of a project team, including designers, owners, suppliers, subcontractors, and more. Project leadership and problem-solving skills are also helpful.

THE JOB OUTLOOK

The job outlook for BIM managers is good. According to the Bureau of Labor Statistics' *Occupational Outlook Handbook*, employment of computer and information technology occupations, which includes

BIM managers, is projected to grow 13 percent by 2026. This rate of growth is faster than the average growth rate of all occupations. "BIM is a challenging, new and exciting career. There is a shortage of BIM people within the construction industry, so there are plenty of openings for those who are keen," said Mitchell. Candidates who have strong technology skills and experience in BIM processes will have the best prospects for landing a good BIM manager job in the construction industry.

CHAPTER FIVE

USING VIRTUAL REALITY IN CONSTRUCTION

Virtual reality (VR) was introduced to the world as a tool for gamers. Wearing a VR headset, people can immerse themselves into a digital world while playing their favorite video games. The popularity of VR means that one thing is clear—the virtual reality revolution is here. However, VR is being used for more than just gaming. One area that is already being impacted by these technologies is construction, from the architect's desk to the construction job site. VR technology has become an increasingly important part of the construction process.

Across the country, construction companies are incorporating technology into their operations. VR is a computer-simulated environment that allows a user to interact in a realistic way within an environment. By moving their head, the user can see up, down, and side to side.

Constructing a building is a time-consuming and expensive task. Once a building starts to go up,

Construction industry professionals wear virtual reality headsets at a construction site. By moving their heads in different directions, they can look at the virtual project from different angles.

problems in the design that are difficult to detect on a blueprint can surface. Making changes to blueprints in the middle of a project can cause a host of problems, from getting new permits to ordering new materials. Even a small design change can have a ripple effect on other areas of the project. Using VR in construction can save time and money on a project.

VR technology offers a solution to this problem. VR can bring blueprints to life before construction even begins. With VR, clients and architects can view the completed building from all angles. They virtually walk through the hallways and see flaws or areas that need to be changed early in the project.

One of the largest construction companies in the United States, McCarthy Building Companies, uses virtual reality to improve its design and building processes. The company's clients put on an Oculus Rift head-mounted display to virtually tour buildings during the design phase. Clients can make changes to the building design quickly and easily before actual construction begins. For example, when designing the Martin Luther King Multi-Service Ambulatory Care Center in Los Angeles, doctors and nurses wore VR headsets and gave the construction company suggestions on details such as where to put equipment in rooms. Mike Oster, chief information officer at McCarthy, said it is critical in a hospital for physicians and staff to be able to reach equipment easily and keep patients satisfied. "Even seemingly simple decisions like where the equipment connections are located on the wall behind the bed, where a trash can is located, how wide the gaps are between beds, or what furniture goes where can be extremely important," said Oster in an article for *Fortune* magazine. Oster said using VR to make these design decisions early enabled them to avoid expensive changes later.

Some construction companies are also using VR to train workers. A construction site can be a dangerous place to work. As such, training for job site safety is critical. The more practice and experience workers can get in a controlled environment—before they are

Oculus Rift is one type of virtual reality headset used by people in the construction industry to give clients a virtual preview of a building project.

in the field—the safer they will be. With VR, computer simulations create realistic environments. Workers navigate the virtual environment using controllers that give them the feeling of operating real power tools and other equipment. VR training environments can also create unexpected job site situations that required split-second decisions, such as what to do if scaffolding collapses. Although VR technology is still in the early stages, it is quickly becoming an exciting tool in the construction industry.

AUGMENTED REALITY

Augmented reality (AR) technology is similar to VR, but unlike VR, it allows the user to see superimposed information of his or her surroundings in the user's view. This provides additional data but still allows the user to interact with the actual environment.

One example of AR technology in construction is the DAQRI Smart Helmet. When worn at the construction site, the helmet allows workers to see their building plans or BIM model as they work, without needing to refer to paper documents. Looking through the helmet's visor, workers see the BIM projected across their field of vision. As they walk through the construction site, they can see the heating ducts, water pipes, and more from the BIM. They can peel back layers of the model to see the building's structure and insulation.

Some users have likened AR technology to having X-ray vision. Using AR, construction workers can find problems faster and make better informed decisions in the field.

WORKING AS A VR DEVELOPER

A VR developer is a software developer that specializes in building VR applications. In the construction industry, VR developers create the applications and platforms needed to run VR technology for training, project walkthroughs, and more.

Typically, VR developers design, test, and develop VR applications that meet customer or company needs. Often, they begin by talking with customers or company executives to see what they need and how they plan to use the application. Through these discussions and other research, VR developers determine the core functions, content, and features required in the application. With this information, developers design the application. In some positions, VR developers write the code for the application themselves. Other times, they give detailed instructions to programmers who write and test the application code.

Virtual reality developers work to not only build the software that construction companies use, but also to keep it updated.

VR developers also test and tweak the design to make sure it works as intended. They may manage user testing and feedback. They also provide general support to users to ensure the VR applications works properly on a wide range of devices and platforms.

Growing up with a love of computers and video games, thirty-year-old Jesus Noland said that working as a virtual reality developer for EON Reality, a VR software development company, is a dream job. Noland creates technology applications to train workers in a variety of industries. "The best thing about working in this field is being able to solve creative problems on a daily basis—it's a lot of fun, actually," he said in an article on CNBC.com.

HOW TO BECOME A VIRTUAL REALITY DEVELOPER

Most VR developers have at least a bachelor's degree in computer science, software engineering, or a related field from a four-year college or university. While in school, students should build a strong foundation in coding and video game development, taking courses in C#, C++, programming, product design, video game design, 3D modeling, animation, and design theory. VR developers should learn and master at least one of the main VR engines created to produce VR apps such as Unity, Unreal, or WebVR. "Using one of those engines is required as those tools will speed up the development process a lot," said developer Maciej Szczesnik in an article for *Techworld*.

Throughout their careers, VR developers must continue to develop their computer skills and stay current on new tools and programming languages. Many students complete an internship at a software or VR company to gain hands-on experience in software and VR development. Some people enter the field by first working as computer programmers or software developers in the gaming industry.

While not all VR apps are used for gaming, working in this sector can teach a person valuable skills, which they can then apply to VR apps in other industries such as construction. "I think most people start with traditional games and switch to VR afterwards. Most of the techniques and processes are very similar on both fields," said Liron Shalev, cofounder and chief technology officer at Halo Labs in an article for *Techworld*.

In addition to strong computer skills, several additional skills are important for people working in this career. VR developers for the construction industry should be knowledgeable in the industry so that they can understand their company and customers' needs. Developers should also be creative, have good analytical skills, and be detail oriented. Developers should also have excellent communication and interpersonal skills. Many developers work closely with others on a team. They must be able to communicate effectively with team members.

THE JOB OUTLOOK

The job outlook for VR developers is strong. For example, EON Reality founder Dan Lejerskar says that his 250-employee company is looking to hire an additional 110 employees in the next year, as the demand for VR and AR products increases.

According to a recent International Data Corp. report, worldwide revenues for the VR and AR market are expected to increase by 100 percent or more over the next four years. Total spending is projected to top $215 billion by 2021. The industry's explosive growth means there will be a lot of opportunities for qualified developers. Applicants with programming skills, who have experience in VR and AR applications, modeling, and creating 3D environments will have the best opportunities.

CHAPTER SIX

USING DATA IN CONSTRUCTION

In every industry, companies are collecting, processing, and storing enormous amounts of data, thanks in part to more powerful computers. Today's computers have more available storage space and can process data faster because of the incredible speed of modern computer processors and internet connections. In addition, new technologies have introduced a huge number of devices that are connected to the internet—from smartphones to car navigation systems. As a result companies around the world, including those in the construction industry, are turning to data analytics, the process of examining raw data to increase productivity.

HOW CONSTRUCTION COMPANIES USE DATA

In the construction industry, huge amounts of data come from the plans and records of anything that

With more data than ever being generated from past and present projects, companies can benefit from harnessing this information and presenting it in useful and meaningful formats.

was built in the past. Additionally, new technologies are enabling companies to collect data on projects in process, from on-site workers, equipment, cranes, earth movers, and even buildings themselves.

To make sense of all their data, construction companies are turning to data analytics. Using powerful computers and analytics programs, businesses can identify patterns and relationships in data and use that information to help them make immediate decisions. This leads to more sales, reduced costs, more efficient operations, and more satisfied employees and customers.

Construction firms are using data in several ways. In the design phase, data can be used to determine what to build and where to build it. For example, Brown University in Rhode Island used data analysis to choose where to build a new engineering facility to optimize student and school benefits. When construction starts, data from weather, traffic, and community activity can be analyzed to determine the best timetable for construction activities.

Data sensors on construction equipment can show when equipment is active and idle, which can reveal valuable information about whether to buy or lease equipment and how to use fuel most efficiently. Data from sensors built into buildings, bridges, and other structures enables companies to monitor performance and conditions. Sensor data can also help companies track energy use in large buildings and develop energy conservation plans. Some companies are

Data sensors on construction vehicles can gather valuable information on usage, which can increase efficiency.

also using data collected from sensors to schedule maintenance tasks as needed.

Ohio-based construction company Nick Savko & Sons Inc. added thirty six global locator devices to its earth-moving and road-surfacing machines so that it could monitor each machine remotely.

The devices gathered data on machine cycle time, idle time, productivity, and more. The data was uploaded into an asset management software program. Data analysis told managers if too many trucks were on site or too few. Data analysis also

CUTTING STEPS, INCREASING PRODUCTIVITY

Before 2016, construction workers at Skanska USA usually walked an average of 6 miles (9.6 kilometers) each day at the job site, just to get the correct building materials, tools, and equipment to the right place at the right time. Then the company began to track worker location and movement data with wearable devices, along with worker-provided data on daily activities. Data scientists and software experts analyzed the data so they could optimize where objects were physically placed at the job site where workers were constantly moving. By putting workers, tools, and resources in optimal positions, they were able to reduce worker's walking distance by about 2 miles (3.2 km) and increased productivity by about an hour per worker each day.

produced information about the number of loads carried, cycle times, and cycle distances. Managers were able to compare actual fuel usage to targets to see if the machines were being used efficiently or if mechanical problems were causing an increase in fuel use. By using the data gathered in the field, the company was able to make better decisions and improve its productivity. Using the data, it finished its project a month ahead of schedule and was able to address problems before they became costly. Going forward, the company plans to use the data to help it better price and plan construction projects.

WORKING AS A DATA SCIENTIST

Companies in every industry, including in construction, need data scientists to make sense of all the data they receive and put it into a useful and understandable format. They use their skills in math, statistics, and computer science to gather and organize enormous amounts of data. Then they use analytical skills and industry knowledge to find solutions for the business. A data scientist writes algorithms to analyze large amounts of data. They build predictive models and software to help a company make decisions about equipment usage, scheduling, job costing, and more.

Each day, a data scientist may perform a variety of tasks. They extract huge volumes of data from a variety of sources. They operate sophisticated analytics programs and statistical methods to prepare data for predictive modeling. They use software programs to cleanse data, which means eliminating irrelevant information. They examine the data from different perspectives to identify trends, opportunities, and weaknesses. They create algorithms to solve problems and build tools to automate work. They also prepare reports that communicate their findings and results for management.

Some jobs will focus more on data analytics—collecting, processing statistical analyses of data, and using the information to answer questions and solve problems. Other jobs require data scientists to build massive databases for big data information. They develop, build, test, and maintain these databases and data processing systems. Once these systems are built, data scientists can use them to access specific data for analysis.

HOW TO BECOME A DATA SCIENTIST

Most data scientists have a master's degree or PhD, in addition to a bachelor's degree. They often major in areas such as mathematics, statistics, or computer science. Taking courses in math and statistics prepares students to work in data scientist jobs. These courses can help students develop the technical skills they will need in linear algebra, calculus, probability, statistical hypothesis testing, and summary statistics. In addition, students should take courses to develop machine learning, which

Students studying to become data scientists may take several classes in mathematics and computer science.

is the science of programming computers that can "learn" from data.

Computer science skills are critical for data scientists. Potential employees need to be able to work with data through such processes as data mining, cleaning and munging (transferring data into a more usable format), and data visualization. They should also be proficient in programming languages, such as Python, C/C++, Java, and Perl. They should be skilled in working with SQL databases and database querying languages. In addition, data scientists should develop skills to work with cloud tools such as Amazon S3. Because the computer science environment is always changing, data scientists must continue to develop new computer skills and stay current on new tools and programming languages.

In addition to strong technical skills, several additional skills are important for people working as data scientists. Data scientists working for construction companies should be knowledgeable in the industry so that they can understand their company and customers' needs. Problem-solving skills are also important because data scientists have to create new ways of looking at and analyzing data. They should have excellent communication and interpersonal skills. Many data scientists work closely with others in a team. The work is often spread among team members and the ability to work well with others and communicate is essential. In addition, data scientists must be able to communicate effectively with management and others who may not have a technical background.

THE JOB OUTLOOK

The job outlook for data scientists is strong. According to the Bureau of Labor Statistics' *Occupational Outlook Handbook*, employment of computer and information research scientists is projected to grow 19 percent by 2026. This rate of growth is faster than the average of all occupations. In construction, this growth is driven by the rapid increase in data collection by companies and a resulting increased need for data-mining services. Computer data scientists will be needed to write algorithms to help construction companies understand large amounts of data. With this information, companies can make their operations more efficient and productive.

Many companies report difficulty finding these highly skilled workers. Therefore, the job prospects for data scientists is good. Candidates who have strong technical and analytical skills in the most up-to-date programming tools and languages will have the best prospects for landing a good data scientist job in the construction industry.

CHAPTER SEVEN

WEB DEVELOPMENT AND DESIGN

With the growth of the internet, all businesses, including those in the construction industry, require state-of-the-art websites. Potential customers visit a construction company's website to learn more about its services, past projects, and clients. They research information about completed projects and read case studies. Having a website is an important way to get a company's work in front of customers. However, just having a site is not enough. Construction companies need to make sure their sites are well-designed and user friendly. Some of the most effective business websites incorporate common features such as graphics, videos, and other practical applications.

Web developers create specialized, eye-catching websites for companies in all industries, including the construction industry. Web developers often play with color, images, layout, photos, and fonts to create a design that will sell. This may include pictures of

A web designer works on a laptop to design the layout of a new construction company website, experimenting with color, photo, and text placement on the page.

completed projects, case studies to highlight the company's work, customer testimonials, and more. Some construction websites have secure pages where customers can log in and view the details and status of a project while it is in process.

Because every company is different, web developers work with each company to create an individual design that appeals to its customers. Web developers then take their design and create a website. After the site is built, they adjust or add updates to the site regularly.

When ARCO Construction, a St. Louis-based construction company, felt that their website was as good as it needed to be, they hired the Timmermann Group, a web design firm, to redesign it. Web designers at Timmermann began the project by performing an in-depth analysis of the existing ARCO website. They reviewed data about the site's performance and identified strengths and weaknesses. They talked to company employees about the areas they wanted to improve on the website. The design team identified specific content for the site that would improve a user's understanding of ARCO's brand and encourage them to interact online with the company.

The web designers determined that information about completed projects, along with awards, honors, and testimonials, significantly improved potential customers' opinions of the company. The design team worked to highlight this information for users and make the site easy to navigate. The completed redesign features a comprehensive gallery of ARCO's finished projects in a card-style layout, which website visitors can easily navigate.

DEVELOPING WEBSITES FOR THE CONSTRUCTION INDUSTRY

Web developers design and create websites. They are responsible for the site's appearance and its technical features. These include the site's performance or speed, and its capacity, which is the amount of user traffic it can handle. Some web developers also create content for sites.

In a typical day, a web developer might meet with clients or co-workers to talk about the function and design of a website. They write code for sites, often using programming languages such as HTML, CSS, and JavaScript. They create and test applications for the site. They work with other team members and designers to determine a site's information, function, and layout. They incorporate graphics, audio, and video into the site. Once the website is up and running, web developers monitor traffic, make adjustments or additions as necessary, and troubleshoot any problems.

An illustrator uses a graphic tablet, which allows her to hand-draw images and graphics with a special pen-like stylus.

Web developers customize websites for a customer or company's needs. Different types of websites need different applications to work correctly. For example, a construction company's site might have a section where clients can check on a project's status. Working with the rest of the product development team, the web developer determines which applications and design work best for the site.

While some web developers handle every part of a website's construction from design to maintenance, others specialize in certain areas. Back-end web developers focus on how a site operates. They oversee the website's technical construction. They create the site's basic framework and make sure that it works as designed. Back-end developers also determine the process for adding new pages and information to the website.

In contrast, front-end web developers focus more on how a site looks and how users interact with it. They create layouts and integrate graphics, applications, and other content. Front-end developers often write web programs in computer languages such as HTML or JavaScript. Once a website is up and running, webmasters maintain and update them.

BECOMING A WEB DEVELOPER

Most web developers have at least an associate's degree in web design or a related field. For more technical jobs, some employers want employees to have at least a bachelor's degree in computer science, programming, or a related field. Taking courses in graphic design can also be helpful, especially if the web developer will be involved in creating a website's visual appearance.

Web developers should have strong technical and web programming skills. They must be proficient in HTML, the markup language for making web pages. Developers should also have strong technical skills in other programming languages such as JavaScript and CSS and be able to work with multimedia publishing tools such as Flash. Because the computer science

CERTIFICATION AND LICENSING

Although web developers do not need any special licenses, undergoing training or getting certifications can improve a person's chances of landing a job or getting promoted. Certification courses, training seminars, and courses organized by professional societies and universities can show a person is committed to improving his or her knowledge and skills. Common web development certifications include certified web developer, certified internet webmaster, advanced web developer, and mobile application development.

environment is always changing, web developers must continue to develop new computer skills and stay current on new tools and programming languages.

In addition to strong technical skills, web developers should also have several other qualities and skills to be successful. Because web developers often spend a lot of time at a computer writing lines of code for hours, the ability to concentrate and focus on small details is extremely important. A tiny error in the HTML code could cause an entire webpage to stop working.

Successful web developers are often very creative people, which can help them design a website's appearance and make sure it is innovative and fresh. Web developers should also

```
function AvviaTrasmissione
    document.Pagamento.
    document.Pagamento.
}
function AvviaContrass
    document.Pagament
    document.Pagamen

7
,8
39      </SCRIPT>
40      <TITLE>
41
42      </head>
43      <body leftmargin='
44      <form action=".../
45      <input type="hid
46      <input type="hi

        <center>
        <br><br><br>.

                    <%strin
```

Web developers use Hypertext Markup Language (HTML), the language used to create the part of websites that users see and interact with.

have excellent communication and interpersonal skills to communicate effectively with coworkers, management, and clients.

THE JOB OUTLOOK

The job outlook for web developers is excellent. According to the Bureau of Labor Statistics' *Occupational Outlook Handbook*, employment of web developers is projected to grow 15 percent by 2026. In addition, the growing use of mobile devices will increase the number of opportunities as developers will be needed to create sites that work on mobile devices and multiple screen sizes. Candidates who have strong technical skills and knowledge of multiple programming languages and digital multimedia tools will have the best opportunities for working as a web developer in the construction industry.

GLOSSARY

architect A person who designs buildings and in some cases also supervises their construction.

blueprint A design plan or technical drawing.

certification An official document that shows a level of achievement.

cloud computing The practice of using a network of remote servers hosted on the internet to store, manage, and process data, rather than a local server or a personal computer.

contractor A person or company that undertakes a contract to provide materials or labor to perform a service or do a job.

data analytics The science of examining raw data and drawing conclusions from the information, often to increase the productivity of a company.

database A set of data held in a computer.

engineering A branch of science and technology that deals with the design, building, and use of engines, machines, and structures.

immersive Generating a three-dimensional image that appears to surround the user.

internship The position of a student or trainee who works in an organization, sometimes without pay, in order to gain work experience.

infrastructure The basic physical and organizational structures and facilities needed for the operation of a society or enterprise.

mobile app A computer program designed to run on a mobile device such as a phone, tablet, or watch.

processor A part of a computer that performs calculations and manipulates data.

productivity A measure of the efficiency of a person, machine, factory, or system.

sector A part or subdivision of a society or an economy.

sensor A device that detects or measures and responds to input from the surrounding physical environment.

subcontractor A business or person that carries out work for a company as part of a larger project.

virtual Not physically existing as such but made by software to appear so.

Associated General Contractors of America (AGC)
2300 Wilson Boulevard, Suite 300
Arlington, VA 22201
(703) 548-3118
Website: https://www.agc.org
The AGC is the leading association for the
construction industry. AGC represents more than
26,000 firms, including over 6,500 of America's
leading general contractors, and over 9,000
specialty-contracting firms.

Association of Software Professionals (ASP)
ASP Executive Director
PO Box 1522
Martinsville, IN 46151
(765) 349-4740
Website: http://asp-software.org
The ASP is a professional trade association of
software developers. It provides a community for
software developers to share information about
the industry.

**Canada's Association of Information Technology
Professionals (CIPS)**
60 Bristol Road East
Unit 8 - Suite #324
Mississauga, ON L4Z 3K8
Canada
(905) 602-1370
Website: http://www.cips.ca

CIPS represents thousands of professionals in the
Canadian IT industry and provides networking
opportunities, certification of IT professionals,
accreditation of university and college programs,
and an IT job board. The organization also advocates
to the Canadian government on issues that affect the
IT industry and professionals in Canada.

**CompTIA Association of Information Technology
Professionals (AITP)**
1120 Route 73, Suite 200
Mount Laurel, NJ 08054-5113
(800) 224-9371
Website: https://www.aitp.org
CompTIA AITP works to advance the information
technology profession through professional
development, education, and national policies.
It features webinars, conferences, awards for
professionals and students, a career center with
a jobs board, and networking options that are of
interest for computer science professionals.

**Construction Management Association of America
(CMAA)**
7926 Jones Branch Drive, #800
McLean, VA 22102
(703) 356-2622
Website: https://cmaanet.org
CMAA promotes the profession of construction
management and the use of qualified construction
managers on capital projects and programs.
Membership in CMAA includes more than four

thousand firms and individuals, including owners, engineers, architects, contractors, educators, and students.

Information Technology Association of Canada (ITAC)
5090 Explorer Drive, Suite 510
Mississauga, Ontario, Canada L4W 4T9
(905) 602-8345
Website: http://itac.ca
The ITAC supports the development of a digital economy
   in Canada. It represents information technology
   professionals in a wide variety of industries.

FOR FURTHER READING

Abraham, Nikhil. *Coding For Dummies* (For Dummies). Hoboken, NJ: John Wiley & Sons, 2016.

Bedell, J. M. *So, You Want to Be a Coder? The Ultimate Guide to a Career in Programming, Video Game Creation, Robotics, and More!* New York: Aladdin, 2016.

Gerber, Larry. *Cloud-Based Computing*. New York, NY: Rosen Publishing, 2013.

Henneberg, Susan. *Virtual Reality*. Farmington Hills, MI: Greenhaven Publishing, 2017.

Kassnoff, David. *What Degree Do I Need to Pursue a Career in Information Technology & Information Systems?* New York, NY: Rosen Publishing, 2014.

La Bella, Laura. *Becoming a Data Engineer*. New York, NY: Rosen Publishing, 2017.

La Bella, Laura. *Building Apps*. New York, NY: Rosen Publishing, 2015.

Lowe, Doug. *Java All-in-One For Dummies*. Hoboken, NJ: John Wiley & Sons, 2014.

Matthes, Eric. *Python Crash Course: A Hands-On, Project-Based Introduction to Programming*. San Francisco, CA: No Starch Press, 2015.

Niver, Heather. *Careers for Tech Girls in Computer Science*. New York, NY: Rosen Publishing, 2014.

Payment, Simone. *Getting to Know Python! Code Power: A Teen Programmer's Guide*. New York, NY: Rosen Publishing, 2014.

BIBLIOGRAPHY

Autodesk BIM 360. "Better Coordination, Fewer
    Clashes." August 25, 2017. https://info.bim360
    .autodesk.com/bim-360-case-studies#ufh-i-
    361510851-better-coordination-fewer-clashes.
Billante, Pete. "Why Your Construction Company Is
    Really in the Business of Construction Technology."
    Connect and Construct, June 28, 2017. https://
    connect.bim360.autodesk.com
    /business-of-construction-technology.
Buncio, Anton Dy. "How Building Information Modeling
    (BIM) Has Revolutionized the Construction
    Industry." ViaTechnik.com, June 9, 2017. https://
    www.viatechnik.com/blog/building-information
    -modeling-bim-revolutionized-construction-industry.
Bureau of Labor Services. "Industries at a Glance:
    Construction." Retrieved March 29, 2018. https://
    www.bls.gov/iag/tgs/iag23.htm.
Burger, Rachel. "10 Ways Commercial Construction
    Companies Can Use Big Data." Capterra
    Construction Management, January 19, 2016.
    https://blog.capterra.com/10-ways-commercial
    -construction-companies-can-use-big-data.
Furlong, Joanna. "A Guide to Technology for
    Construction Companies." Business.com, May 2,
    2017. http://www.business.com/articles
    /construction-technology-software-guide.
Gaudiosi, John. "How this 150-year-old company uses
    virtual reality." Fortune.com, August 25, 2015.
    http://fortune.com/2015/08/25
    /mccarthy-construction-vr.

GoConstruct.org. "Case Study: Building Information Modelling Manager." Retrieved March 29, 2018. https://www.goconstruct.org/construction-jobs/career-explorer/bim-manager.

Green, Erin. "What Is Building Information Modeling?" Engineering.com, February 3, 2016. https://www.engineering.com/BIM/ArticleID/11436/BIM-101-What-is-Building-Information-Modeling.aspx.

Mercer, Christina. "How to get a job as a VR developer: How to become a virtual reality developer." *Techworld*, May 12, 2017. https://www.techworld.com/tutorial/careers/how-become-vr-developer-3658829.

Mortenson.com. "Mortenson Creates First-of-Its-Kind Augmented Reality App for Construction Visualization." July 18, 2017. http://www.mortenson.com/company/news-and-insights/2017/mortenson-creates-first-of-its-kind-augmented-reality-app-for-construction-visualization.

Peterson, Becky. "These are the hottest skills for getting a job in cloud computing." Business Insider, July 6, 2017. http://www.businessinsider.com/these-are-the-hottest-skills-for-getting-a-job-in-cloud-computing-2017-7.

Rogers, Kate. "The virtual reality industry can't stop growing—but supply of workers is limited." CNBC.com, December 8, 2017. https://www.cnbc.com/2017/12/08/virtual-reality-continues-to-grow–but-supply-of-workers-is-limited.html.

Sage Construction and Real Estate. "Cloud Computing and the Construction Industry." Retrieved March 29,

2018. https://www.sage.com/na/~/media
/site/sage-construction-anywhere/responsive
/Cloud_Computing_and_the_Construction_Industry.
United Rentals. "Construction Workers in Demand:
BIM Engineers." January 23, 2018. https://www
.unitedrentals.com/project-uptime/workforce
/construction-workers-demand-bim-engineers.

INDEX

ABOUT THE AUTHOR

Carla Mooney is a graduate of the University of Pennsylvania. Before becoming an author, she spent several years working in finance as an accountant. Today, she writes for young people and is the author of many books for young adults and children. Mooney enjoys learning about new technologies and the impact they will have on different industries and the average consumer.

PHOTO CREDITS

Cover Ndoeljindoel/Shutterstock.com; back cover and pp. 4–5 (background) nadla/E+/Getty Images; p. 5 Viaframe /Corbis/Getty Images; pp. 8, 15, 24, 33, 42, 51, 60 Fuyu Liu/Shutterstock.com; p. 9 Pressmaster/Shutterstock.com; p. 11 Nicolas_/E+/Getty Images; p. 14 Jupiterimages /Stockbyte/Thinkstock; p. 16 Trevor Adeline/Caiaimage /Getty Images; p. 18 Jon Bilous/Alamy StockPhoto; p. 20 ProStockStudio/Shutterstock.com; p. 22 UberImages /iStock/Thinkstock; p. 25 Viewpoint/Shutterstock.com; p. 27 JulieanneBirch/E+/Getty Images; p. 31 dennizn /Shutterstock.com; p. 34 Bloomberg/Getty Images; p. 36 eXpose/Shutterstock.com; p. 37 Solis Images /Shutterstock.com; p. 39 Kzenon/Shutterstock.com; p. 43 Westend61/Getty Images; p. 45 Future Publishing /Getty Images; p. 47 Hero Images/Getty Images; p. 52 S.Dashkevych/Shutterstock.com; p. 53 Falcor/E+ /Getty Images; p. 57 wavebreakmedia/Shutterstock.com; p. 61 Milindri/iStock/Thinkstock; p. 63 wavebreakmedia /iStock/Thinkstock; p. 66 atm2003/Shutterstock.com; interior design graphic (abstract circuit) Titima Ongkantong /Shutterstock.com.

Design: Michael Moy; Layout: Nicole Russo-Duca; Photo Researcher: Sherri Jackson